Sweet Insurgent

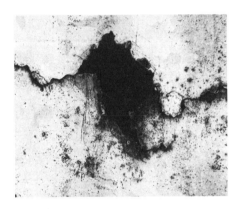

Elyse Fenton

saturnalia books

Distributed by University Press of New England
Hanover and London

Sweet Insurgent

Elyse Fenton

Distributed by University Press of New England
Hanover and London

Saturnalia Books
105 Woodside Rd.
Ardmore, PA 19003
info@saturnaliabooks.com

ISBN: 978-0-9980534-0-0
Library of Congress Control Number: 2016952335

Book Design by Saturnalia Books
Printing by McNaughton & Gunn
Cover Photo: Shawn Johnson
Cover Design: DJ Murphy

Author Photo: Jo Ann Santangelo

Distributed by:
University Press of New England
1 Court Street
Lebanon, NH 03766
800-421-1561

Poems from this book were originally published in the following journals:

American Poetry Review; Copper Nickel; Cream City Review; Fogged Clarity; Hubbub; Hoppenthaller's Congeries; Narrative; New Welsh Review; Portland Monthly; Prairie Schooner; Raleigh Review; Salamander; Southern Humanities Review: Sou'wester; Zyzzyva.

Table of Contents

For Mira,
my sweetest insurgent

I

The War Ends

Offstage, if it ends at all. No broken
hydrants, no tongue-kissing in the streets.

It's not often I think *fuck the classics*
but what passes for mercy is Achilles

finally offering up a tortured corpse.
All day the sky's sitting its own shiva,

grainy groveling in place of cloud & everyone
I never knew is coming home. Last night

Hektor's draggled body was the deer
caught & sideswiped on the coast road,

mange tinseled, only electric misfirings
to keep the creature upright though

it tried to sit. Zip-tied prisoners do that.
We are so much smaller rage doesn't

end us so much as make the suffering
messier & more easy to abide. Homer

doesn't bother with the lesser graces:
the prayer of lineament or Priam's fingers

gone catfish on the body of his son. Stand
at the roadside long enough you become

dirge, a woman with a washcloth in her hand.

The Chain

Maybe inside all our bodies is the fine body
        of an ultramarathoner   a body that needs

to be lubricated against itself   that needs
        to be doggedly watered and hand-fed

and salted periodically with tablets no
        bigger than the sori of a fern   that just

needs the steel-banded calculus of trust
        to take it and take it good   the body   yes

your own soft body leads by a leash   rocks
        flanging the dark pines   the body

your body jerks to a stop in the rough
        clearing   hands on shoulders on knees

on unblessed ground   the body your body
        sledges with rusted stakes through the palms

heels nipples   that drives a chain rippling
        through the intestines with the blindness

of water approaching the dam   blindness
        of boys at the edge of the woods cinching

themselves into some dusty unnameable
        shape   threat or surrender with its parallel

sides   toward a voice with a sledge
        in its hands and a chain in its teeth calling

come and get it brother   come and get it

Artificial Eyeball

Jimmy's new app for predicting
      migraines is more than tea sludge

passing for truth but who wants
      a lesson in the sovereignty of data

the moment before summer
      lightning squats down to tongue

the kiddie pool or lighter fluid
      knights a strand of hair?

Because I tend to let possibility
      hold forth one lifetime too

many when the test for Tay Sachs
      came back maybe my body came up

soothsayer, new hands begging
      offal and hot coals, nerve endings

forking razor-stripped filaments
      like the gold thread holding

the remnants of the 5000-year-old
      eyeball nested in its artificial eye.

Archaeologists say it was made
      of bitumen paste for lightness,

worn by a six-foot tall Arabian
      priestess exalted and perpetually

feared. Abscess translated to blossom
      where her socket skin all day touched gold.

Preparations for the Kingdom

All night you must be carrying something:
brush hooks, bent ladders, the dredging

engines of your hands. Or else casting
a line out along the inner banks of my flesh

for whatever creosote fin-flash muddies
the shallows I'll never know. You are in-

terior's interior, a darkness the dark-
ness hides behind and yet here I am

in any winter tundra, in any failing or
fallen empire: haphazard lean-to, twig

and raveled twine, haywired compass still
holding its salt-ravaged needle true north–

Wild Deer

They come down from the hill wilds overnight, three wild deer
drawn to the morning glory'd wire of our lives, our rows

of plenty drawn between the spanse of scrub and road.

In the deer pen of my mind the wildest thoughts nose through
the scurf to nibble juniper, forget what green desire brought them

here. More timid than their summer kin October deer step

soft-shod through the frosted noose of breath that ropes
each hornless head. How easily they start and scare. How easily

I turn from them before the sun-gilt leaves they hungered for

leave them starved of any thought but home. No gentling I know
will lead them out. They'll lunge themselves to death by a neighbor's

buckshot or a broken neck. But first they'll eat their fill.

Notes on Labor

The mattock knows rock by name
          at least enough to sweet talk an opening
in the conversation, to manipulate

          weight over distance with the help
of friction or its lack—*Honeyhips,*
          Granite, won't you scoot on down—

unlike dynamite, which speaks
          only incendiaries in its catechism
of fracture– powder's shotgun-marriage

          to flame– which is still more than I can say
of the lodged boulder you've become,
          second sun now going down over

the stubborn hills, lead cloak of cold
          I can't drape around me without dry-
heaving and cursing the weft of it

          your staggering winter-weight. How
did I not learn the dialect of rupture
          all those weeks sledging rock to gravel

above tree-line? Even in sleep my body
          knew rubble's incantation was no last
word, just the hunger of bones for their own

          splintering, the clamor of flesh for its make-
over in stone. Dante must have felt
          the talus beneath his feet quail like dinner

plates at the Last Supper but let's be
    honest: you're hardly more than a windfall
of scree. Your father skipped the stone

    I sent him across the lily-scudded catch-
ment of Saddam's palace because that was
    the only body of water at hand. When he finally

laid flesh upon me again we were infinite
    as glaciers ransacking a moderate slope. Now
I'm trying to labor the way they tell me,

    as in, efficiently, as in the summer I gutted
a chimney from roof peak to cellar hole, trampling
    an eon of brick dust and lathe through the lintels

of a stranger's house until I could stand in the base-
    ment's bedrock and see up through the empty
shaft we'd unbuilt a few scattered cinders of sky.

Brief History of Picasso

You are my grotesque: a *Demoiselle d'Avignon*

in miniature, tail in place of mask, skull a furred

corona stolen fresh from horror films. Picasso

wanted to name it *Brothel* so we would see it

in plain sight. Bridge-girder thighs, spectrum

of flesh tones suppurated red: how not to read

in such defiance, grace? Your eyespots spill wide

inside me, our blood-slick sea. Look to Guernica

when you're able. A bull wears a crown of horns,

a man is birthed or rent from barrel shards. A bomber

has always just exited a contrail-gored sky. Oh my

loveliest unlovely! Name the barrel *agony*. Name the bull

nameless. Tail turned to fire though the testicles remain.

Small Collection for Baby with Pushpins and Hairlock

The days stretch equinoctial and flat as fields
of sorghum. Always that falling or flying feeling
though the ground is solid as scarab as fruit cake
as the small sturdy bones in your ear called *canal*.
If you were a boat, the story goes, I'd be wind. I'd be-
friend raven. I'd be a ravening. Hell, I'd carry you
home in the beak of my bones as I carried you here.
Long dura of days. Long re-gifted graft. Gravity
we say and mean undoing. Mean grave. Tractor
trough you enter as if into water. Gorse to the ears.
If I am a raveling you are my *rave rave*. A perpetual
splintering. My most tempestuous thread.

Sweet Insurgent

Outside the flesh the wind's a hinge
broken both ways. Some forms
of breakage cause no real harm
but that's not why we're here. *Pathei*
mathos says Aeschylus, we suffer
into knowledge, but what if we only
suffer into dumb surprise? *What*
what? What what? say the rotors
of my friend's helicopter just before
going down, rotors without lift, rotors
more heart murmur than murmur-
ation, but after impact he opened
the door & walked away. Hello
tenacious earth. Sometimes
you have to practice crying uncle
for years to make it stick.
Maybe because I don't want to be
sliced open I covet interiors, make
your address – also my own –
untouchable: Dear Hidey Hole, Dear
Den of Snakes. I even covet the hazard
music of your hands, their rain-on-
flashing, their morse'd every other note
pried up. In the Harm Disposer's
Handbook not every bomb can be
dismantled so it must stay buried,
one good ear bent & ticking in the dirt.

II

The Empire

Across history courtyard swans
knit their tongues from fallen skeins

of blood. Before the Great Wall was
the idea of the Great Wall. So great

the workers' bodies fit ambered
inside, bootlaces and spines

intact as the border between two
warring countries. The blindness

comes only after the spangling darkness
wears down, a neckful of light drained

from the wings and jagged snapped-off
beaks of the swans prying at the ancient

masonry for a kernel, a button, a fist
broken in the shape of a swan.

Forms of Protest

All month long police in riot gear
crowded the city like novitiate whales

learning the trick of baleen. Of all
the underwater currents never mind

the one that's going to turn. A mother
I know just buried her son but that's only

an expression. She had him turned
into ash. Easier to imagine the big peace-

able bodies of whales – their cargo,
their bioluminescent wattage –

than a mother's attendant grief. A hunger
so vast the whole goddamn ocean pours

black & guppied & vigilant into your throat.

Cry It Out

Not sleeping will kill you but we do it

 anyway, drone armies mapping our scalps

  as we read the obituaries and mourning doves

  chew the leaded sill. Because I am no good

 at making my child sleep I know I will someday

have to beg the stoic trees to be dismissed

as late as possible while time leaves its shit-

 kickers by the stairs and strops into some

  eternal leather the first hackneyed syllable

  of my name. We've always misread the heart's

 pneumatic quickening and why not. Kudzu

wheels in another vengeful decade. Two fists

 pour their frantic hollows into the door.

Training

October totals itself like a rusted station
    wagon into a tree. I used to think I could run faster

in the dark but it's only that I become less visible
    to my own myopic pain. Each lap the little white

dog shitting itself into some autumnal oblivion
    in the yellow leaves is just a bough bending

to contemplate exactly as much nothing
    as possible, a version of agony ghosting the oaks

for some more pliable self. I still can't feel
    my limbs even begin to contemplate nothing.

In the likely phony but long enduring myth
    of the Inuit, elders ripped off their clothes

and left the village when it was time to die.
    Eventually I'll run off all my inhibitions

about slowness, learn to admire the grim inertia
    of the villagers who knew by heart the pickled

nakedness of their beloveds receding like snow
    geese toward a dull crease in the hills.

Night Feeding

Night rehearses its midnight sanctions and we
follow. Come hill in high water. Come with your
dominion of hunger built brick by brick by tongue.

At this hour we are charnel fodder: you with your
heat-seeking Icarus cloak and me with my pocketful
of fallow. If I were your ox-cart driver, would you

untether me for slaughter? Would I be your baffle?
Would I be your wig of thorns? Your wings fit
precisely in my beak and your mouth is the word

for the sound of a swallowed stone. Here they are,
my sweet, my starveling: my milkless bones
                              come ripe for barter.

Sing

The favorite fowl are dead, coyote-grabbed and beheaded
within the wire and the coyote dead from shot and the mess

of them carved down a cradle of hard pack for the roundworms

to carpenter clean. Child, your lullabye's a shovel croon.
Mesquite be my headstone, creosote my everlovin' roost.

Life on Other Planets

Thanks to old science fiction
we've been thinking about it

all wrong. Mile-wide colonies
with their gaudy odalisques

and breast shaped domes,
inhabitants who speak some

Turkic-Altaic variant from
beneath their silver kaftans.

But by *habitable*, astrophysicists
just mean capable of holding

water. By *life*, celled organism.
Maybe that's what my friend

means when she says she's
not sure anymore what life

can be. Her child is two weeks
dead. In the galaxy's audition

the planets keep rotating
redly, saying *pick me, pick me.*

Babel

This morning we're Babel before the fall.
    No dialect. You're speaking wind-swabbed
plains, ball moss on oak. A bell. A still

    snowless sky. The voice of lantern-lobbed
darkness, a keyhole of cloud, the best last
    spell to break back the cold. Speak the bit,

the brace, the bitten-through lip. Sassafrass
    blooming through well and grave like the bit-
umen black lobes of dawn. So what if Babel

    fell. I've got your voice like a ziggurat's got
its domeful of stars, nighthawks scalloping Ls
    in the sky. God is rubble. Is a tongue wrought

from sand. Open your mouth and there's
    wind, there's rain. Mud ramparts slipping
down the skinned rungs of your name.

When You Begin Asking About Your Provenance

I'll say all hail the fine non-leaded tip breaking itself
       like a railroad spike against the census page I'll
               say

blessed be the box checked and unchecked all the boxes
        checked the box labeled south-anglo-asian/
              ashkenazi-saxon

brown-white really light-cocoa-pink a helix strand-
        stripped & re-equipped like cufflinks the steel
             coupling

of trains the soft box of the brain kelp-waving half
       above water half breath-held beneath or else
              sub-

merged meaning less than merged as in the blood's art-
       erial traffic the slow rolling stop the cops love

to catch as if the veins were filled with the trembling light
        violations of leaves– sycamore maple black
             birch–

annealed to limbs like sprung padlocks the palmed
       self pressed exactly half against sky *Barn-*

doored climbers say meaning to strip sideways lose
        balance a kind of falling away one-half at a time

as if we were made entirely of halves and not this burl-
       esque village of cells this thatch-roofed
            commune

of cells the house of us a house only mitotically divided
the lease co-signed as if love were a lease as if
love were

the least harm we could think in this world to
do—

Surrender

Any wild thing can wound if it's scared
enough – the lesson of the fawn
in the cistern, the possum in the street.

But when reassurance opens my mouth
the lies arrive like mountain goats come
down off the ridge to lick the crystallized

salt of our piss from the rocks. What animal
stops there? The man who held three girls
captive for years lasted a few weeks in prison.

Even now, no one has invented a name
for the child carried up from the basement
in the ambulance driver's arms.

Micro

In the world beneath us ants fight
single drops of rain. To understand
the maddening strength of surface tension

try opening a plastic package of batteries
with your teeth. What can I say about war?
Two ants are better than one; their fighting

helps them lift and brace the lanterned orb
up to their sophisticated jaws to drink.
Who knows how long a drop will last

an ant, how long before the rain. Already,
my unbearable thirst is back.

A Stranger Says My Husband Must Want to Return to War

Tonight teeth in the weeds

loosen like the clamshelled

tops of jugs and the elegy

unwrites itself. Out past

the sea-wall: a beaker of waves

brought back from boiling.

Who still believes in harm-

less? Egrets know to hunt

the keloid shore, the brute

years to drag themselves home.

Again, Spring

Flagpole or war ship, the first
purple asparagus drills its blunt
rigging through the dirt.

You want to say *worship* this—
but it's relentless, like the first time
you stick your finger down

the baby's throat. How wrong
to believe you are dislodging death.
You, the god who put it there.

Repent

The dumb thing I said comes back
to dismantle the house, poor dredged

brain with its banging doors and hinges
halved to sheer the sky. Swallows traffic

the opposite way toward the chimney, orange
construction cones lift toward some second-

ary heaven. Air turns back from smoke
to air. Big chain-link mouth, big weeping

tongue: sutures only temporarily intact.
If I know I have my whole life both loved

and spoken with precisely the wrong
kind of restraint, why stop now, water

rising against the sill, blue tarp flagellating
roof beams with its last good wing?

Vasectomy

Maybe it's better you can't feel the universe

casting the ninety-six percent of itself that is dark
matter across the threshold—tractor trailer turning

left across traffic, rotten whale dynamited into rain

—but you can feel, can't you, afternoon refusing
to steady its half-ladle of light against the glass, body

within your body chucking its clothes into the well.

We're No Robert Capa Photo

Sweet fellowship of field. The troughs embrace
our thighs like shields. Your body buttoned neatly

into shade. Say, Once was soldier, those were the days–
they weren't. Serrated sky to sawgrass our sight.

Once were blades. Once crowbarred back the night's
facade to see how we were skeined. The light of us

a fist. A derelict scrap of earth the mortars missed.

III

Human Shield

I was ready when you wanted me

               shadow-polished severe & human

as a lie. Forgive me the one stray

               hair, unbidden skin, unwillingness

to turn toward a lens. You said

               innocent victim so I was beckoned

from hearth trash & poplar, blind

               linen & a run of rubbled-shut weeks.

Even as you began to read I was

               slipping slim rations, kevlar rungs

into the sleeve of each rib & rubbing

               cinders into the oilcloth of my face.

How else did you think you'd find me

               but lacquer-blacked & bandoliered

inked back to the vernacular just after

               you'd looked at me and looked away?

...The account di-	*verged* the paper says
lifting all ballistic trace	from the man's palm
unthreading carbide lead	·freeing wholesale each
finger from its gun-	slung fist A practiced
erasure A sleight	of hand Oldest carnie
trick in the book	The way a sawed- through
woman can be par-	layed back to flesh & sequins
no smoke or suture	but the slow reveal–

*

On my back I'm barrowed and brim   easily with falling particles:

pear blossom   cartridge hail   rain.

*

Compound, botanically, means two leaves

$\qquad$ opposing, some green divergence of the
$\qquad\qquad$ self

anchored at the same stalk whereas

$\qquad$ medically it's the bone broken from casement

or housing if you believe the body

$\qquad$ is a house. Believe the body is the body

and see where it gets you: Kevlar-

$\qquad$ Spined Goddess of Guardpost & Wait.

Lay out the map. See how compound's

$\qquad$ divergence comes to mean home. Dusty
$\qquad\qquad$ tillage

& aphids in the bitter orchard, three stories

$\qquad$ of concrete & a crooked holding pattern of

$\qquad$ smoke rising from trash fire like a
$\qquad\qquad$ pried-

$\qquad$ free soul—

*

First I learned to shimmy my lithesome self my lonesome
                              down a cave wall's cubby hole

                    for kicks. Went tree bole, became the pigeon-
                                                    nymph's

assassin song. Rats like whetstones I'd shear up against

                    and shine. Whatever got left down there in the batshit

& drudgedust, in the bone hangar couldn't protect me

                    from the armor already mine.

*

Remember the fishbowl not the fish.

A two-way mirror gone dark

on one side like the habited self grown

hard as river glass. Look anywhere.

Beyond all good theories of heaven

are banks articulated with razor wire

& stones that won't stop skipping–

*

Double tap, the technique goes, meaning

                  one bullet to the head, one to the heart –

tin can, tin can – to catch the body's kilter

                  and train it out, but I have methods too.

Take a zero with its gut sickled back

                  to spine. Now tilt. Here's where to cower.

Hollowed gourd, hubcap, horn stripped

                  of plenty. Do we ever really learn how

mercy ends. If I have to, I can wait. I can

                  hold this naked pose for years.

*

Interrogation Report

To be grammarian I had to learn   the interrogative   a sentence
asking for reply   crowbar for a skeleton key   a strategy to unbolt a jaw

I memorized subordinates until   a stall technique   they chinked
my tongue   Good grammar means good sense   a colon like a latex glove

You have to know the rules to break   but that's a lie
      You have to know the way to give up   only teeth

*

As long as I'm in the protection business, I'd rather be

        Athena's personal Gorgon. Let go the temperance

and grow my hair snakelicious golden, build a wall-

        eyed frieze to commemorate my already frozen

tongue. While I'm at it, come close. Take off

        your lens cap. Forgetting means you'll learn to manage

your losses. The worst part isn't blindness

        but the lack of news. All-day static like a sonic cut-

lass licking its blunt way through blighted groves.

Close enough to touch but not all there.

Only air kiss and shadow. A practice

in Plato. In the myth of the turtle hoisting

the world I'm nothing but ether, sub-firmament's

clutch of soot smoke and ozone, a division

between matter and meaning where someone's

always failing to translate the air. If ever

there was no heaven, I'm there.

*

Give

The thing never

        learned was loose-

                ness

how to be supp-

        led like

                wind

slipping the door's

        under-

                bite

salt softened

        bit

                the hand's

strop

        a tongue

                come

        quick

                undone

*

Take

You will scan news

            for my name and not think

Santa Lucia   not think Joan of Arc

rinsed from saddle by the wet plume

of God's hand

           Take the *ah* of the mouth

a bullet will forge in the flesh of a calf

then the sound of blood   holding still:

                 Amal

meaning expectation: Monday

sky before Black Hawk   before

world steepled in

           Don't think

           the bed was never made

*

Interrogation Report

So many holes   the wind rides in
decamps   lays out a spread

I'm a picnic

in ant smoke & gingham
bloody with afternoon sun

No crumbs

That's the way it is until the end
Someone's sardine fingers

plugging ears
the tussle of soup bowls

& improbably
                 the rain –

*

Dear Next of Kin,

I was not the armor only   you
I wielded like no danger that

I know   I had to   messy unclawed
no bright mechanism at work you

were the sloppy work   you
my reel of sand   my sovereign state

Oh Leda knew   Mother of a God/
But Not   how will I bear Not You

the syrupy river dark the lantern you
spliced from flame I cannot bare

limbs without armor   sorrow tree
without bark   the banks beneath you

rebar concrete where the geese were you
were prey   once sat   still shit   Oh pray

you do   Oh white-wash me   I can-
not   leave without you—

*

Best to think of me as the body
                    unbodied   Closer to alloy than the imperfect seam-

weld of muscle to bone All skeletal trace
                    of tenderness ligamented loose by smelt or flame

As if it were possible to bear no memory
                    of matter: less onion skin than cello-

phane caul unsuppled by air But maybe
                    you begin to see me best by not looking

the way you have to throw back the loose
                    tarp of the sky to summon a few artless stars

or the heart's fugitive mechanics hot-
                    boxed beneath a wire-thumbed breast Not quite

a drowning in plain sight because I've been
                    working on my posture: keystoned

tensile the right curvature for tempered
                    steel but otherwise elegant flexible & amen-

able to order: believe me when I say
                    I always understood rule number one *Don't think*

yourself impermeable to mean be just
                    permeable enough–

*

Derelict as a loose atom, a coaster

of sun staining all the woodwork red.

Dove sheaf and shovelful, gas rising

hydraulic through yeast. How a body

can be leavened & loosed: a bee farm

a broken loaf or less. The sparrow-torched

air where eaves meet soffit and end.

IV

Bear in a Tree

I dream of helicopters circling
the lost tribe, traffic patterns
mapping out a newer vein of grief.
The toast burns, but not the way
I intended. The bear stays treed.
Living on earth in the age of the 6th
Extinction just means more extra-
vagance all around. Tourists
of Destruction, we're here to buy
sunshades, microscopes, decorative
wall mounts for extracted honeybee
wings! But say the bear outlasts
the traffic, outlasts the tree.
Say the helicopter never touches
down. This voice in my throat
when you kiss my face: both claws
and hooves pulped on the rocks
of the last unflooded canyon floor.

Catfish

When the new pope kneels to wash
the brown foot of a female inmate, the world
sets its flashbulbs to rupture. Already, spring's
trundling out its clutter, blossoms from the new
ornamentals manufactured to leave
no unsightly gaps in the air. My daughter begs
to see the dead animals in the supermarket,
the dead crabs, the dead pigs, dead the appellation
for the whole caste of meat posed in its naked
créche behind the glass. The bacon, I tell her,
the veal? Complicity can crease the tongue
back on itself like a smashed origami dog
or a prisoner missing the cold assurance
of pliers in her mouth. So much survives
tenderness you have to believe it.
Even the live catfish float serene as light
bulbs in their blue chemical baths.

Sand

Once I showed up to a party with a sheep skull

strung around my head, teeth heroic along the seam

of my scalp, fence barbs rusted into a cauterized

wound. When the night was over a perfect thimble

of sand slipped from the empty socket. It's possible

to lose all but the last decibel of history –

already the microphone so far away we get reverb

like an impersonal act of kindness, dice in the lake

bottom twenty yards down. Four percent of the sand

at Omaha Beach is made of shrapnel. Also quartz,

feldspar, limestone, iron, rock, shell and somewhere

in there: bone. I try to imagine the work of the micro-

scope as a process of illumination but my eye keeps on

with its rich taste for destruction, splintering images,

wicker lawn furniture into 6-pack ribbons and dune.

Catastrophe, the eye's keepsake! In her pockets

the child keeps acorns and invisible snow. When

she shucks her clothes, sand spills from her cuffs, egrets

wing from a far colony. We keep our clothes and teeth

and hair longer than our flesh but sand, old lackey

keeps the rest. When a migraine pours its lash of oil

into my ear, the sedimentary record sloshes, a battleship

scrapes its landing gear on the history of glass.

Red Lion

The old tricks don't work. The lying in wait,
the come hither mitts plaster-knit too large to be
of harm. *We are left alone without excuse*, says
Sartre, who has been left alone not long enough.

Red Lion, you're a fixed point behind the flaking
gate, both nostrils painted shut. Some lives
are like that. A little girl calls you kitty and lays
a bottle cap on your head: Goodbye, ferocious

world. Aren't you always the first one begging,
Lord, don't let me outlive my only face–

Greed

The neighbor's sprinkler is just life support,
set midday to soak the sidewalk and the dying
summer grass, but it makes my daughter shriek.

I always thought I'd be first to heed the mercy
kill but I can't even keep the kitchen shears sharp.
Now preservation of her laughter's what I'm on

about, which is how the dahlias live another week
to lie their crooked necks against the dullest blade,
which is how the slivered naked moon gets its right

to privacy revoked. Amber cicada shell with its empty
hooks still honed: I never planned to love like this.
I was the girl in the yellow bathing suit who climbed

bridge railings to court the extra foot of air, old-timer
outside the St. Helens guard station knifing his own
truck tires just before the mountain disappeared.

Quarantine

The child says it like some kind of winter
        flowering tree whose twisted scarlet buds

you'd have to gather with pliers
        by their skirts as light begins to lose itself

at sea. Sometimes a sentence drifts away
        like a knit shawl in a canal but here

she's busy lining magnets on the fridge
        while fever shakes its frost-burnt leaves

across her face. The only canal I've ever
        known was in Mongolia, frozen solid, limned

with human shit. Each time I ran its banks
        I'd catch the gravestone carver leaning back

against his granite stack of blanks. Some days
        I can't remember lonely like that. *Quarantine*

she says, not Latin, forty port-bound days
        for foreign ships and not the false root *core*,

fist of seeds locked inside a stent but *choir-*,
        somehow Southern, choir-, stumbling nomad

from one sound to the next, palmful of sweet-
        drunk hornets clubbing an apple at the heart.

Sweethearts,

Let's be a little less brave together
say the zinnias to each other, heads

like olive frittatas sliding unbroken
across the pan. Down the block

it's chickens chickens and a ruminant
wind bringing autumn back into

the equation. Choose instead
the tractor's absence, bankruptcy

of hives, the universe bending down
to pull a thread from its cuff

and flash a third row of teeth. Figs
gyrate into light's densest coil

so the sugars coalesce, wine stain
into bruise, prow into broken

waves. Fist into throat. When I said
we should love with more fury I meant

even the laryngial crows, even the kleenex
thrashed in the laundry to lace.

The Dinosaurs of My Youth

Keep coming back with new configurations
of armor and bone, feathers for scales, car-
nivorous accessories glinting a fine digital
light. Already I miss the Mesozoic, the era
before the meat eaters' gamesmanship

when dinosaurs were the size of chickens
cowering in bull rushes and tar pits and all
it took to rule was a few thousand alligator
ancestors flexing their average-sized tails
and flashing the dirty dinnerware of their

teeth. But if destruction has so many names
we ought to know at least a few. Now it's so
long Brontosaurus, hello Argentinosaurus,
Shantungosaurus, a whole new taxonomy
of sauropods. In the four-year-old's

theory of extinction one dinosaur touched
something hot—volcano or stovetop—and
another and another until the heat spread
and they all burned up *from the inside*. Maybe
she's wrong about extinction but right

about desire, the exercise in mass die-out
we practice for our tamer selves. What I saw
last night when I closed my eyes the moment
before you made me come for the third time—
still dragging our ragged unendurable bodies

across the alkaline plains—was not volcano or
ash, crater or spark, not the winging laundry lines
of the last million passenger pigeons in their pen-
ultimate rapture but the fields snowed calf-deep
in shit, moon spitting back its mouthful of light.

Woodlands

Your daughter walks between headstones
on new legs. Head a buoy, body a line
fed down to strafe some restless deep.

Say loneliness is as constant a calculus
as desire. Say there is no restless deep. Over-
head a sick hawk rummages a stripped branch

but don't think: augury. It's just dusk sifting
the ruins. Just your daughter, growing tall.

Independence Day

And the ear's a house with the siding ripped off.

I blacken a skillet of pork dumplings while fire-

works fritter their insect cells against the blinds.

Oh holy day. My husband the veteran slides

the sash down another beer & forgets

to flinch. Outside the last daylit hour the air

burns like the neutered hundred-flair

of a hydrangea, cinder cone tip like every other

mountain around. We come back

in damper variants of ourselves like a form

of vengeance. Wick wetted, a tatter, a spit-back

bone; a chorus digging its slight grave

on our lips. Out beyond earshot the meadow

reaches to finger the singed nettles & foxglove,

the gas lines, the mutilated voles.

NOTE

Human Shield originates with the report – later proven false – that Osama bin Laden used his fifth wife, Amal Ahmed al-Sadah, as a "human shield" before he was killed in the 2011 Abbottabad raid.

**Winners of the Saturnalia Books
Poetry Prize:**

Telepathologies by Cortney Lamar Charleston

Ritual & Bit by Robert Ostrom

Neighbors by Jay Nebel

Thieves in the Afterlife by Kendra DeColo

Lullaby (with Exit Sign) by Hadara Bar-Nadav

My Scarlet Ways by Tanya Larkin

The Little Office of the Immaculate Conception by
Martha Silano

Personification by Margaret Ronda

To the Bone by Sebastian Agudelo

Famous Last Words by Catherine Pierce

Dummy Fire by Sarah Vap

Correspondence by Kathleen Graber

The Babies by Sabrina Orah Mark

Also Available from saturnalia books:

The True Book of Animal Homes by Allison Titus

Plucking the Stinger by Stephanie Rogers

The Tornado Is the World by Catherine Pierce

Steal It Back by Sandra Simonds

In Memory of Brilliance and Value by Michael Robins

Industry of Brief Distraction by Laurie Saurborn Young

That Our Eyes Be Rigged by Kristi Maxwell

Don't Go Back to Sleep by Timothy Liu

Reckless Lovely by Martha Silano

A spell of songs by Peter Jay Shippy

Each Chartered Street by Sebastian Agudelo

No Object by Natalie Shapero

Nowhere Fast by William Kulik

Arco Iris by Sarah Vap

The Girls of Peculiar by Catherine Pierce

Xing by Debora Kuan

Other Romes by Derek Mong

Faulkner's Rosary by Sarah Vap

Tsim Tsum by Sabrina Orah Mark

Hush Sessions by Kristi Maxwell

Days of Unwilling by Cal Bedient

Gurlesque: the new grrly, grotesque, burlesque poetics
edited by Lara Glenum and Arielle Greenberg

*Letters to Poets: Conversations about Poetics, Politics,
and Community*
edited by Jennifer Firestone and Dana Teen Lomax

Artist/Poet Collaboration Series:

Velleity's Shade by Star Black / Artwork by Bill Knott

Polytheogamy by Timothy Liu / Artwork by Greg Drasler

Midnights by Jane Miller / Artwork by Beverly Pepper

Stigmata Errata Etcetera by Bill Knott /
Artwork by Star Black

Ing Grish by John Yau / Artwork by Thomas Nozkowski

Blackboards by Tomaz Salamun /
Artwork by Metka Krasovec

Sweet Insurgent was printed using the fonts
Grotesque MT and Adobe Garamond